Don't Let the Crocodiles Fight!

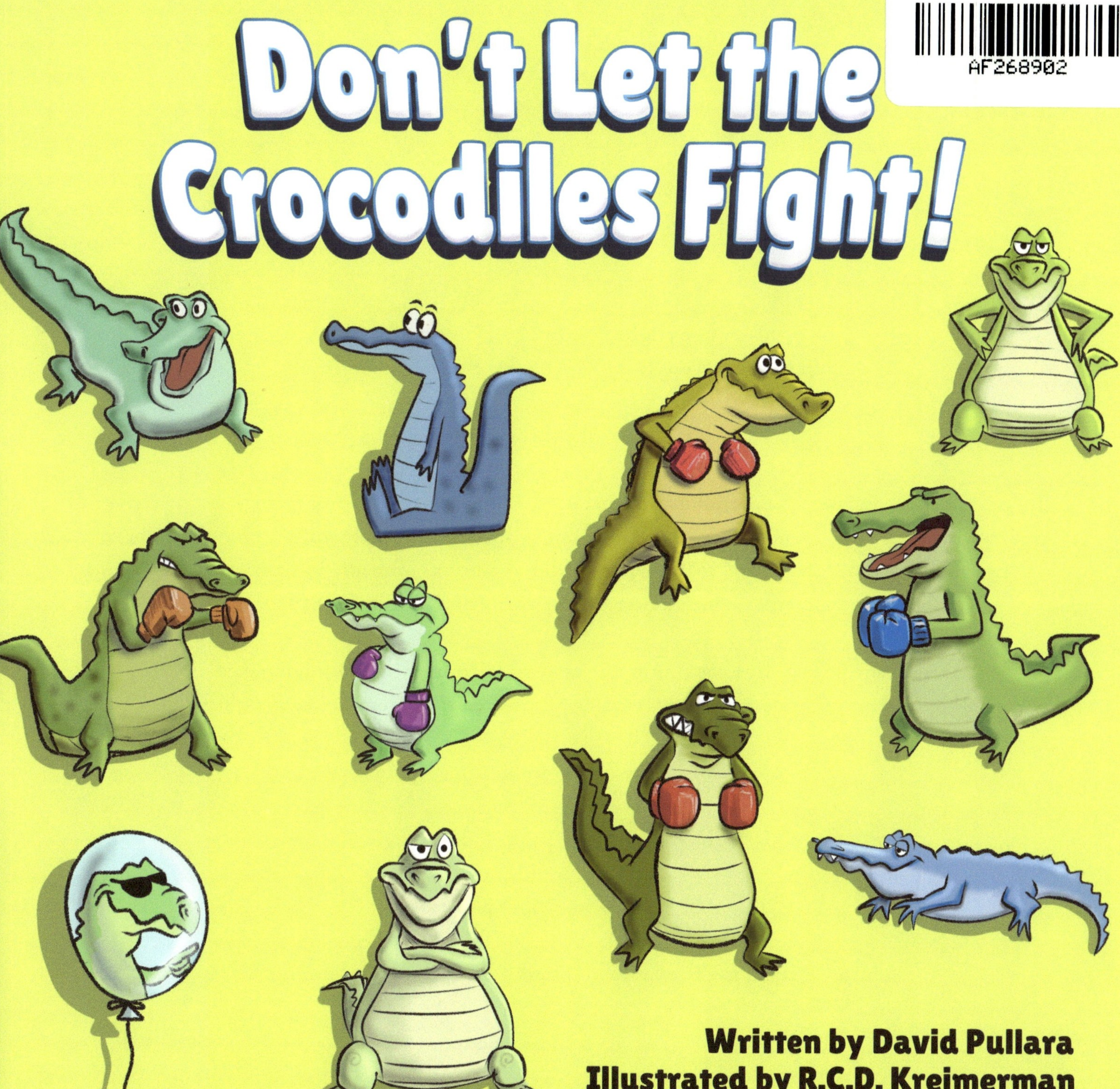

Written by David Pullara

Illustrated by R.C.D. Kreimerman

MINDBURST
PUBLISHING

For Chloë, Aidan, Charlotte, and Andrew:
Your brilliance, creativity, energy, and humour make the world a better place
and inspire me to be a better person. I heart you forever and always. - dp

For Pilar:
Thank you for refusing to let my quirks go to waste. - R.C.D.K.

Good night,
Sleep tight,
don't let the
bed bugs bite!

AND...

Don't let the crocodiles
Fight!

Always be brave and do right.

stop

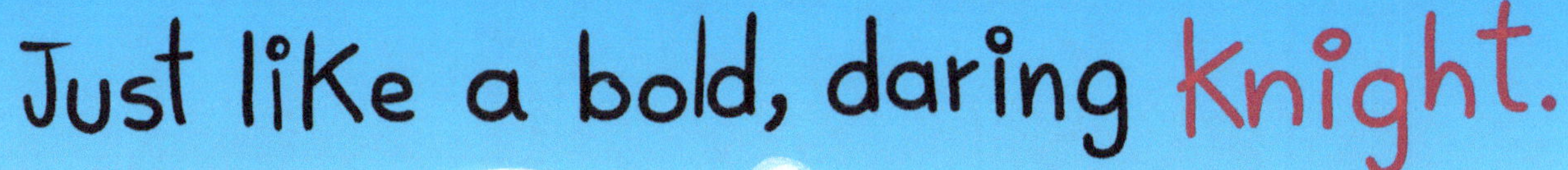
Just like a bold, daring knight.

Riding a dragon
in flight!!

up to a dizzying height!

Down below, there's a pirate in sight...
On a ship with big sails gleaming white.

N
S

In the water that shimmers so bright...
A mermaid sings songs that delight!

And fairies nearby
will unite...

we love
you

to cheer her with
all of their might!

Ki

DS!!!

I don't mean
to be
impolite...

But now I will
turn off the light.

Goodnight
G'night

Goodnight
Nite, nite

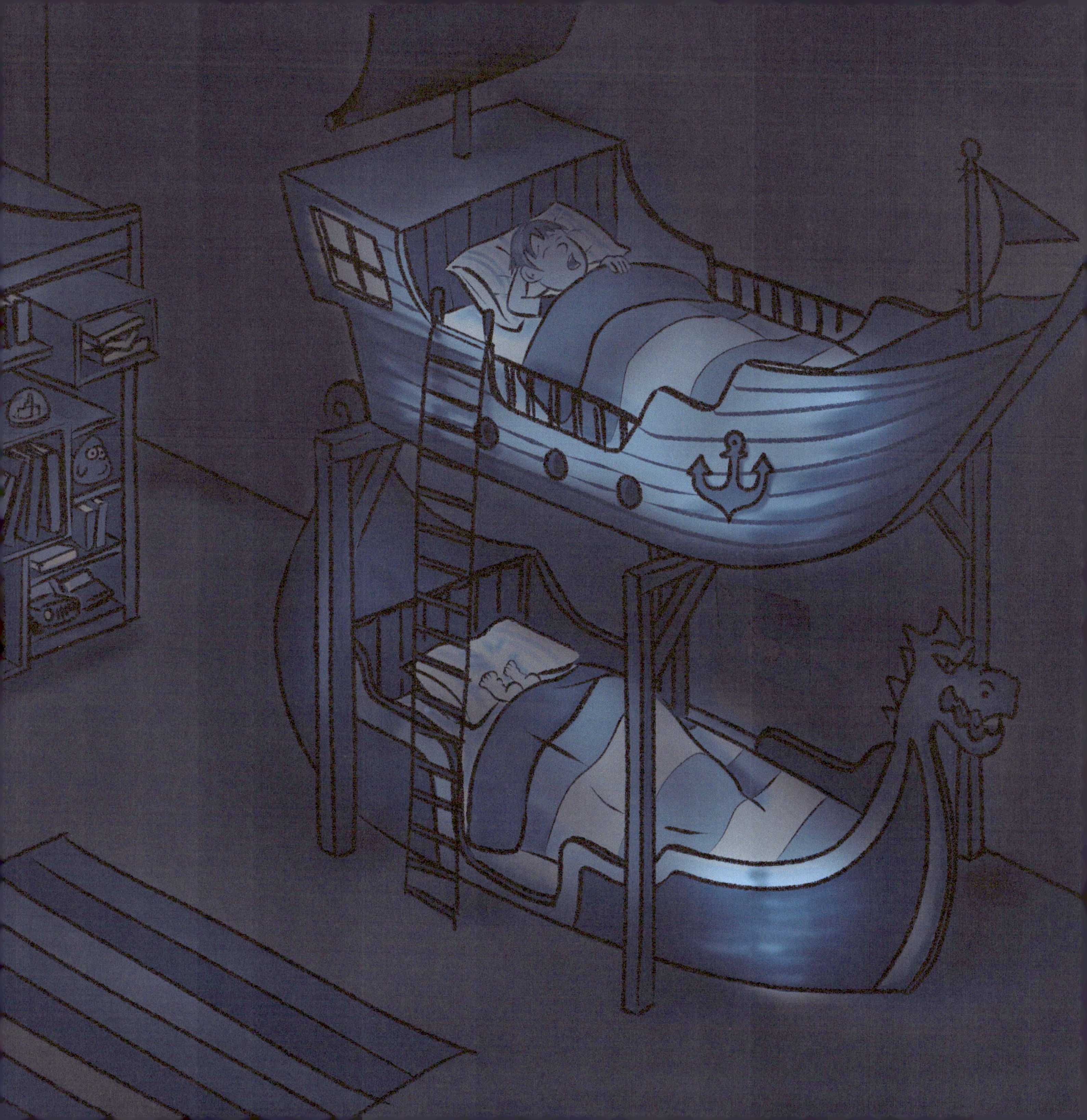

Now our story has come to an end,
But the fun isn't over, my friend!
On the pages that follow you'll find
Some suggestions to help fuel your mind.

Go use them to build your own fable...
It's fun and we know that you're able!
Pick a character then pick a word
Build a story...and make it absurd!

A big dinosaur with a kite?

A fiery dragon in flight?

A purple car that's lost its wheel?

A hippo in search of a meal?

The ideas are endless, it's true...

And the story is all up to you!

Don't ask yourself why, ask "Why not?"

Now go on... let's see what you got!

Magic Shoemaker
Unicorn
Balloon Artist
Wacky Scientist
sweet!
Time Traveller
Firefighter
Treasure Hunter
Jungle Animal Rescuer
Magic Potion Seller
Mime
Wizard

Swimming
Helping
singing
Fighting
Painting
Flying
Exploring
- Sailing
- Searching
- Discovering
- Solving
  (Mysteries)
- Inventing
- Transforming
- Growing
- Learning
- Rescuing
- Building
Dreaming
let the dream continue
Writing
Hiding
Casting (spells)
Climbing
Jumping
Discovering
Running
Playing
Cooking
Dancing
Celebrating

ADD

- Bad
- Clad
- Dad
- Fad
- Glad
- Grad
- Had
- Lad
- Mad
- Pad
- Rad
- Sad

BRASS

- Class
- Gas
- Lass
- Pass
- Crass
- Grass
- Mass

CAT

- Fat
- Flat
- Hat
- Mat
- Pat
- Rat
- Sat
- That
- Vat

BE

- Flee
- Free
- Gee
- Gree
- He
- Key
- Knee
- Me
- Pee
- Sea
- See
- She
- Spree
- Tea
- Thee
- Three
- Tree
- We
- Wee

BOAT

- Coat ✓
- Float ✓
- Goat ✓
- Moat ✓
- Note ✓
- Throat ✓
- Vote ✓

BEER

- Cheer
- Clear
- Dear
- Ear
- Fear
- Gear
- Hear
- Near
- Peer
- Queer
- Rear
- Sear
- Sheer
- Smeer
- Sneer
- Steer
- Tear
- Veer

BUY

- Bye
- Cry
- Dry
- Fly
- Fry
- Guy
- Hi
- Lie
- My
- Pie
- Ply
- Shy
- Sky
- Spy
- Sty
- Tie
- Try
- Why

LOVE

- Dove
- Glove
- Shove

CLAY

- Day
- Fray
- Gray
- Hurray
- Parlay
- Play
- Pray
- Replay
- Slay
- Stay
- Stray
- Tray

AIR

- Bare
- Care
- Chair
- Dare
- Fair
- Flare
- Glare
- Hair
- Pair
- Pear
- Rare
- Square

BAND

- Banned
- Canned
- Fanned
- Gland
- Grand
- Hand
- Land
- Manned
- Panned
- Planned
- Sand
- Scanned
- Spanned
- Stand
- Strand

CAR

- Far
- Bar
- Scar
- Jar
- Star
- Czar
- Tar
- Spar
- Guitar

BED

- Bled
- Dread
- Fed
- Fled
- Head
- Led
- Red
- Said
- Shed
- Shred
- Sped
- Spread
- Thread
- Wed

WHITE

- Bite
- Bright
- Fight
- Flight
- Fright
- Height
- Light
- Might
- Night
- Quite
- Right
- Sight
- Tight

BAIL

- Fail
- Frail
- Hail
- Kale
- Mail
- Nail
- Pail
- Pale
- Rail
- Sail
- Scale
- Snail
- Tail
- Tale
- Trail
- Veil
- Wail
- Whale

SAVE

- Cave
- Crave
- Gave
- Grave
- Knave
- Pave
- Rave
- Shave
- Stave
- Wave

David Pullara is a marketer, consultant, advisor, and university instructor.

With the publication of this book, "children's book author" gets added to the list.

But his most important job is "Daddy" to Chloë, Aidan, Charlotte, and Andrew.

It's the greatest job in the world.

R.C.D. Kreimerman is a data storyteller, aspiring musician, illustrator,

and proud father of Nic and Mat.

Inspired by his sons, he urges them to never lose their sense of wonder about life.